A Note to Pa

DK READERS is a compelling program for beginning
readers, designed in conjunction with leading literacy
experts, including Dr. Linda Gambrell, Professor of Education
at Clemson University. Dr. Gambrell has served as President
of the National Reading Conference, the College Reading
Association, and the International Reading Association.

Beautiful illustrations and superb full-color photographs
combine with engaging, easy-to-read stories to offer a fresh
approach to each subject in the series. Each DK READER is
guaranteed to capture a child's interest while developing his
or her reading skills, general knowledge, and love of reading.

The five levels of DK READERS are
aimed at different reading abilities,
enabling you to choose the books that
are exactly right for your child:

Pre-level 1: Learning to read
Level 1: Beginning to read
Level 2: Beginning to read alone
Level 3: Reading alone
Level 4: Proficient readers

The "normal" age at which a child
begins to read can be anywhere from
three to eight years old. Adult
participation through the lower
levels is very helpful for providing
encouragement, discussing storylines,
and sounding out unfamiliar words.

No matter which level you select,
you can be sure that you are
helping your child learn to
read, then read to learn!

LONDON, NEW YORK, MUNICH,
MELBOURNE, AND DELHI

For Dorling Kindersley
Senior Editor Elizabeth Dowsett
Editor Julia March
Managing Art Editor Ron Stobbart
Publishing Manager Catherine Saunders
Art Director Lisa Lanzarini
Associate Publisher Simon Beecroft
Category Publisher Alex Allan
Production Editor Marc Staples
Production Controller Rita Sinha
Reading Consultant Dr. Linda Gambrell

For Lucasfilm
Executive Editor J. W. Rinzler
Art Director Troy Alders
Keeper of the Holocron Leland Chee
Director of Publishing Carol Roeder

Designed and edited by Tall Tree Ltd
Designer Sandra Perry
Editor Jon Richards

First published in the United States in 2011
by DK Publishing
375 Hudson Street, New York, New York 10014

11 12 13 14 15 10 9 8 7 6 5 4 3 2 1

DK books are available at special discounts when purchased in bulk
for sales promotions, premiums, fund-raising, or educational use.
For details, contact:
DK Publishing Special Markets
375 Hudson Street
New York, New York 10014
SpecialSales@dk.com

A catalog record for this book is available
from the Library of Congress.

ISBN: 978-0-7566-7126-6 (Paperback)
ISBN: 978-0-7566-7127-3 (Hardback)

Reproduced by Media Development and Printing Ltd., UK
Printed and bound in China by L.Rex Printing Company Ltd.

Discover more at:
www.dk.com
www.starwars.com

Contents

FEEL THE FORCE!

Written by Benjamin Harper

The power of the Force

There is a mysterious energy that flows throughout the galaxy. It flows through all living things. It is called the Force. The Force is invisible, but special beings can detect it. They use the Force to gain amazing powers.

The Jedi need to use all their mastery of the Force against droid armies controlled by the Sith.

Two different kinds of energy make up the Force—the light side and the dark side. The light side is used by kind beings called Jedi. Evil beings called the Sith use the dark side. The Sith and the Jedi are battling for control of the galaxy. Who will win? The fate of the galaxy hangs in the balance.

Chosen One
An ancient Jedi legend tells of a Chosen One who will bring balance to the Force. The Chosen One is a young boy called Anakin Skywalker.

The light side

Wherever the light side of the Force is strong, kindness and justice rule. But the light side is not an easy path to follow. Those who want to use it must want to help others. They must be prepared for a lot of hard work and training. To use the light side, beings must have complete control of their emotions. They must never give in to fear or anger—even for a moment. These strong emotions could pull them toward the dark side!

Yoda is an expert at using the Force. He has spent centuries using the light side of the Force to teach others.

Yoda may be small and hundreds of years old, but the energy of the light side makes him a very powerful Jedi.

The Jedi

Thousands of years ago, beings who were drawn to the light side joined together to form the Jedi. The Jedi use the Force to keep peace throughout the entire galaxy and to protect others. They will never use their special powers to attack another being.

However, they do not shrink from battle when confronted with evil!

To help them detect the Force that runs through everything, the Jedi spend long periods of time in quiet thought. This is called meditating.

The Jedi are ruled by a special council made up of 12 of the most powerful Jedi.

The dark side

The dark side of the Force is a truly terrifying power. It draws its energy from strong emotions, such as greed, fear, and hatred. By deliberately stirring up these emotions, beings can use the dark side to become incredibly strong. But they must also be willing to commit terribly destructive acts. Much of the pain and suffering in the galaxy is a result of the dark side.

Darth Vader and Emperor Palpatine use the dark side of the Force to seize control of the galaxy.

The Sith

The sinister group that follows the dark side of the Force is known as the Sith. The Sith use their emotions to tap into the dark side. They can channel its energy to bring about many things they want—and what they want is power! Like the Jedi, they meditate to improve their control of the Force.

The mysterious Darth Sidious is the Sith Master.
He is helped by a series of Apprentices, such as
Count Dooku, who is also known as Darth Tyranus.

Force choking
Count Dooku can use the dark side to choke his enemies. He channels the Force so it squeezes their necks so they can't breathe.

The Sith do not care for other people. They will not hesitate to use the power of the dark side to attack or destroy anyone who stands in their way.

Path to the dark side

Jedi are trained never to give in to their emotions, even if terrible things happen. If they do, the power of the dark side of the Force may pull them in. Once they are in its grip, they can feel so strong that they think they are invincible.

Anakin is so blinded by the dark side that he turns against even his old friend and teacher Obi-Wan Kenobi.

Jedi Knight Anakin Skywalker finds it impossible to control his feelings when he believes that his wife Padmé could die. How is it that the light side cannot save Padmé? He gives in to his fear and greed, and allows the dark side of the Force to take hold of him. From now on, he is no longer Anakin. He has become Darth Vader!

Darth Vader has to wear a special suit so he can breathe.

Training to use the Force

When the Jedi or the Sith have connected with the Force, they use its power to see, hear, or feel what is around them. It enhances their normal senses.

Very young Jedi are called Younglings. While training to use a lightsaber, they wear a special helmet that covers their eyes and blocks out the outside world.

This way, they have to rely only on the Force to sense where their target is. After many years of hard practice, the Jedi will eventually be able to use the Force very skillfully. They will be able to do several things at once—sometimes without moving a muscle!

Younglings practice using a lightsaber under the guidance of a Jedi Knight or Master.

Lightsabers

In battle, the Jedi and the Sith use a very special weapon called a lightsaber. It has a metal handle containing tiny crystals that power a glowing blade of light. The blade can be any color—blue, red, green, even purple.

Only those who can control the Force can build a lightsaber. They meditate over the crystals for many hours.

Jedi Obi-Wan Kenobi shows Luke Skywalker his father's lightsaber with its blue blade.

Mace Windu's lightsaber *Qui-Gon's lightsaber* *Obi-Wan's lightsaber* *Anakin's lightsaber*

Meditation charges the crystals with the Force so they can power the blade. No two lightsabers look the same. Each one is built to be a perfect fit for its user and to suit his or her special style of fighting.

Training lightsabers
Jedi Younglings practice using training lightsabers. These have special blades that will cause only bruises and minor burns.

Using a lightsaber

A lightsaber duel is spectacular.
The blades hum as they flash through
the air, cracking and sparkling as they
clash. Jedi and Sith must stay focused
on the Force during a duel so they can
sense what an opponent is about to do.
They can then use their lightsaber to
block an attack or launch their own.

Obi-Wan Kenobi faces the twirling lightsabers of the evil General Grievous.

Double-bladed sabers

Some Sith Lords use lightsabers with two blades. These are very dangerous! Special training is needed so that the users do not hurt themselves with the second blade.

Mind tricks

Both the Jedi and the Sith can use the Force to influence other people's minds. The Jedi are careful not to hurt or scare people with mind tricks. They will use them only to stop somebody from causing harm, or to create a distraction.

Obi-Wan Kenobi uses a mind trick to sneak the droids C-3PO and R2-D2 past dangerous stormtroopers who are looking for them.

A wave of the hand
To perform a mind trick, the Jedi may wave
one of their hands. This movement channels
the Force into the other person's mind.

The Sith are not so careful, however.
They don't care what harm they cause!
If it gets them what they want, the Sith
will use the Force to go deep into
someone's mind. Then, they can
deliberately channel the energy of the
Force to create fear and panic.

Blocking the Force

Some beings in the galaxy cannot be affected by Force mind tricks.

Any Jedi who try to bend the will of these beings are likely to find themselves being laughed at!

Jabba the Hutt laughs off Luke Skywalker's attempt to use a mind trick on him.

Two species in particular have the power to block a mind trick. They are the Hutts, such as the powerful crime lord Jabba, and the winged Toydarians, like junk shop owner Watto.

Jedi Master Qui-Gon Jinn is a little surprised when his mind trick fails to get Watto to change his mind. The only thing that will work with this Toydarian is money!

Sensing emotions

The Force allows Jedi to tune into another person's mind. They can see images and feel emotions exactly as that person experiences them. They can do this without the other person knowing.

Some Jedi Masters and their pupils use this ability to communicate with each other.

By reading messages or images in each other's minds, they can work together in complete silence. It gives them a great advantage when they are lying low or creeping up on an enemy.

By using the Force together, Obi-Wan and Anakin have developed a strong bond and so they make a good team.

Seeing the future

Some Jedi and Sith can use the Force to see visions of things that have not yet happened. This skill has saved many lives in combat. A Jedi or a Sith can predict what an opponent is going to do next. They can then leap out of the way to safety or they can block an attack with their lightsaber.

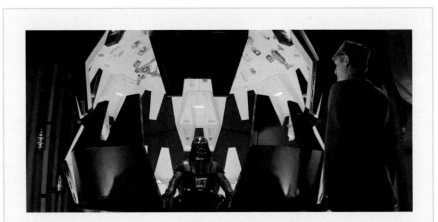

Meditation
To meditate, Darth Vader enters a special chamber. It has a life support system and is the only place where he can remove his helmet.

*Yoda teaches the skill of farsight to Luke Skywalker.
Luke is then alarmed to see his friends Han and
Leia in trouble on the distant planet of Bespin.*

The most powerful Jedi and Sith
spend many hours meditating on the
Force. They are then able to see events
that will happen far away. This skill is
known as farsight.

Moving objects

Imagine being able to move things without touching them! Some Jedi and Sith are able to do just that. They can tap into the Force and use its power to lift an object. They can spin it, pull it to them, or send it crashing into an enemy. This can be very handy in combat.

Showing off
Anakin Skywalker
misuses the Force to
impress people. He lifts
a pear from a plate in
front of him and sends it
floating across the table.

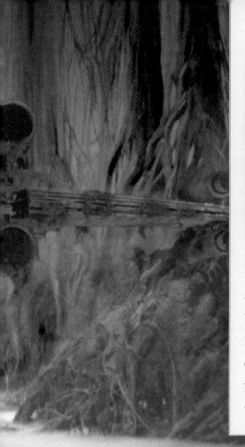

Jedi Master Yoda uses the Force to
lift Luke's enormous X-wing starship
out of the swamps of Dagobah.

A Jedi can use the Force to pull
battle droids onto a lightsaber, or scatter
them out of the way. For those who are
really skilled in controlling the Force,
the size and weight of the object does
not matter.

Agility

Both Jedi and Sith can channel the energy of the Force through their own bodies. When this happens, muscles grow stronger and reactions become lightning-fast. Qui-Gon and Obi-Wan use this skill to race away from a group of deadly droidekas, or destroyer droids, when they are cornered on board a droid control ship.

Jedi and Sith can combine this ability with their skill in anticipating another person's moves. They can then quickly spot an attack and react to avoid it. They can jump out of the way of a blow or raise their lightsaber to block a laser blast.

Obi-Wan uses all of his Force agility to leap out of the way of Darth Maul's flashing lightsaber.

Force jump

By channeling the energy of the Force into their legs, a Jedi or Sith can increase their strength. They can then leap to unbelievable heights or across huge distances. They can use this ability to spring into battle or jump away from an attack with incredible speed.

To an opponent, it may look like they appear out of nowhere and disappear just as suddenly! Force jumps are a favorite skill of Yoda. He leaps about during a battle so that he can confuse and defeat much larger opponents.

Obi-Wan and Qui-Gon use a Force jump to leap across a huge chasm to chase the Sith Lord Darth Maul.

Force deflection

If the Jedi or the Sith are attacked while they are unarmed, they can still defend themselves, so long as they tap into the Force. It allows them to throw up a protective wall of energy that will deflect or block anything, from a laser blast to an avalanche of rocks.

They can then push the objects away from them—or even back at their attackers! Yoda may be small in size, but he has no problem stopping falling boulders. He can even stop Senate seats that are thrown at him by the evil Emperor Palpatine.

Yoda stops a cascade of rocks that are brought down on him by Sith Lord Count Dooku.

Force disturbances

Some Force users are so sensitive that they can detect another Sith or Jedi. They are so aware of the Force's energy field that they can feel ripples in it. These ripples are created when another Sith or Jedi is nearby.

Darth Vader is distracted when he senses the presence of his old Jedi Master, Obi-Wan Kenobi.

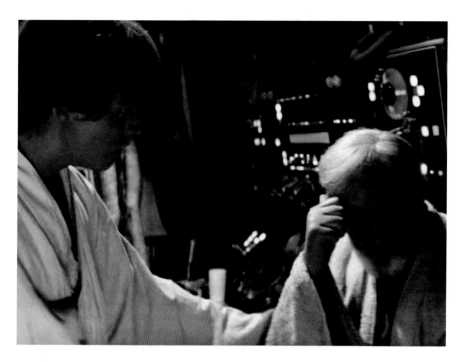

Obi-Wan staggers back when he senses the destruction of the planet Alderaan by the Empire.

Bad or upsetting events may cause shock waves strong enough to make a Jedi physically recoil. A really terrible event, such as the explosion of a planet, will send such a great disturbance crashing through the Force. This can be so powerful that it can almost knock the Jedi off their feet.

Force lightning

By tapping into the destructive dark side of the Force, the Sith can gain deadly powers. They can channel the energy of the dark side through their bodies and send it flashing from their hands and fingers like bolts of lightning.

Any unsuspecting Jedi zapped by these powerful lightning bolts might find their life force being drained before they are able to do anything about it! If they act quickly, they can use Force deflection to block a Sith lightning attack.

Yoda is so powerful that he can block Force lightning and shoot the energy back at the attacker.

Force stealth

Stealth means doing something secretly, without being found out. The Sith use a power called Force stealth to remain undetected by Jedi, even when they are in the same room! They do it by blocking the ripples they create in the Force's energy field.

Palpatine is one of the most powerful Sith of all. By using Force stealth, he has been able to work in the galaxy's government without the Jedi suspecting him! He has even become Chancellor, the leader of the Senate.

The Emperor
Palpatine has no need to use the Force to hide once the Jedi have been defeated. He takes control of the galaxy and declares himself Emperor.

Force ghosts

When Jedi die, their life energy does
not die with them. It lives on, becoming
a part of the Force's energy field.
It is possible for a Jedi who has died
to appear as a Force ghost. As a Force
ghost, they can send advice to a living
Jedi in times of crisis.

If their bond with the Force is very strong, they can actually appear before another Jedi. After he was killed by Darth Vader, Obi-Wan was able to talk to Luke, advising him to use the Force to destroy the Death Star. He even appeared in front of him to tell Luke to visit Yoda on Dagobah.

Restoring the balance

With the Sith in control, the Force becomes unbalanced. The galaxy is plunged into a terrible war and planets are destroyed. What hope is there now? It looks like the stories of the Chosen One will not come true. Anakin has turned to the dark side, and nobody else can bring balance back to the Force.

Vader and Palpatine try to persuade Luke to turn to the dark side of the Force.

The effort of killing the Emperor destroys Anakin's protective suit. With his last breath, he asks Luke to remove his helmet.

It is the galaxy's darkest hour. But in one moment, everything changes. When Emperor Palpatine tries to kill Anakin's son, Luke, Anakin kills the Emperor. He turns back to the light side, ending the dark side's reign. Anakin has brought balance back to the Force and restored peace, just as the stories told. But will the Sith rise again?

Glossary

Apprentice
A person who is learning how to use a skill or power.

Avalanche
A large amount of rocks that fall to the ground.

Chancellor
The person who leads the government.

Chosen One
A special person who will defeat the dark side and bring balance to the Force.

Dark side
The part of the Force that is used by the Sith for evil.

Deflection
A change in the direction of a moving object. The Jedi use the Force to deflect objects.

Droid
A robot. Droids come in all shapes and sizes.

Duel
A fight or battle between two, or sometimes three, people.

Emotions
Feelings a person has, such as anger, happiness, or sadness.

Emperor
The person who rules an entire empire on his own.

The Force
A mysterious energy that flows through the galaxy.

Galaxy
A large collection of stars and planets.

Invincible
Something or someone that cannot be defeated.

Jedi
Beings who use the light side of the Force.

Jedi Knight
A Jedi who has studied under a Jedi Master and has passed the Jedi tests.

Jedi Master
A Jedi who has performed an exceptional deed or has trained other Jedi.

Lightsaber
A swordlike weapon. A lightsaber has a blade of pure energy, and is used by both Jedi and Sith.

Light side
The part of the Force that is used by Jedi for good.

Meditating
Spending long periods of time in quiet thought.

Mind trick
Using the Force to make people do something.

Sith
Warriors who use the dark side of the Force.

Stormtroopers
Soldiers of the Empire. They are commanded by Emperor Palpatine after the defeat of the Jedi.

Youngling
A Force-sensitive child who is trained to use the Force. After taking many tests, a Youngling may become a Jedi Knight.